SIMPLE STEPS TO SNARE DRUM

A COMPLETE METHOD FOR INDIVIDUAL OR CLASSROOM INSTRUCTION FOR THE BEGINNING SNARE DRUMMER WITH AN INTRODUCTION TO BASS DRUM, CYMBALS, TRIANGLE AND TAMBOURINE.

By Anthony J. Cirone

© 1991 Belwin Mills Publishing Corp. (ASCAP)
All Rights Assigned to and Controlled by Alfred Publishing Co., Inc.
All Rights Reserved including Public Performance. Printed in USA.

INTRODUCTION

SIMPLE STEPS TO SNARE DRUM is a beginning snare drum method designed for very young students without previous training. If the student has had some musical training, some lessons may be omitted. These step-by-step lessons also provide information on proper equipment, holding the sticks, the correct way for striking a drum, and a systematic progression for introducing basic elements of drumming.

Material is presented clearly and is easy to understand; each lesson adds additional information. Musical examples are presented allowing the student to master new techniques or note values.

As the lessons progress, musical signs and instructions, including simple dynamics, are explained enabling participation in a school band or orchestra.

This method teaches the student to play in 2/4, 3/4, 4/4, 5/4, 6/4, 6/8 and Cut-Time, taking them through quarter, half, whole, eighth, sixteenth-notes and rests.

There is an introduction to the proper playing techniques for bass drum, crash cymbals, triangle and tambourine. The students may perform these instruments during classroom instruction. Each solo has bass drum and cymbal parts written on the first space; the triangle and tambourine can double the snare drum line (omitting the flams).

SIMPLE STEPS TO KEYBOARD PERCUSSION and SIMPLE STEPS TO TIMPANI should be introduced, which will complete the student's instruction in total percussion.

I hope my love for drumming and the education process is communicated to both teacher and student throughout these pages.

A.J.C.

ILLUSTRATIONS BY MARK P. BONFOEY

*** TABLE OF CONTENTS ***

Page #

STEP ONE - Selecting The Proper Equipment 4
STEP TWO - Holding the Sticks 5
STEP THREE - Single Strokes 6
STEP FOUR - Double Strokes 7
STEP FIVE - Improving our Stroke 8
STEP SIX - Combinations of Single and Double Strokes 9
STEP SEVEN - Learning to Read Quarter-Notes 10
STEP EIGHT - Quarter-Rests 12
STEP NINE - Bass Drum 14
STEP TEN - Snare Drum Solos 16
STEP ELEVEN - Half-Notes and Whole-Notes 18
STEP TWELVE - Crash Cymbals 20
STEP THIRTEEN - Drum Solos 22
STEP FOURTEEN - Dotted Half-Notes 24
STEP FIFTEEN - Eighth-notes 26
STEP SIXTEEN - Drum Solos with Eighth-notes 28
STEP SEVENTEEN - The Snare Drum Roll 30
STEP EIGHTEEN - Drum Solos with Rolls 32
STEP NINETEEN - The Triangle 34
STEP TWENTY - The Flam 36
STEP TWENTY ONE - The Flam Tap and Flam Accent 38
STEP TWENTY TWO - Six-Eight Time 40
STEP TWENTY THREE - Drum Solos in Six-Eight Time 42
STEP TWENTY FOUR - Drum Solos with Rolls and Flams 44
STEP TWENTY FIVE - The Tambourine 46
STEP TWENTY SIX - Cut-Time 48
STEP TWENTY SEVEN - Snare Drum Solos 50
STEP TWENTY EIGHT - Sixteenth-Notes 52
STEP TWENTY NINE - Final Snare Drum Solos 54

STEP ONE

*** SELECTING THE PROPER EQUIPMENT ***

Snare Drum Sticks:

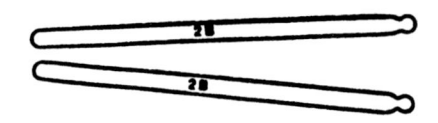

Practice Pad:

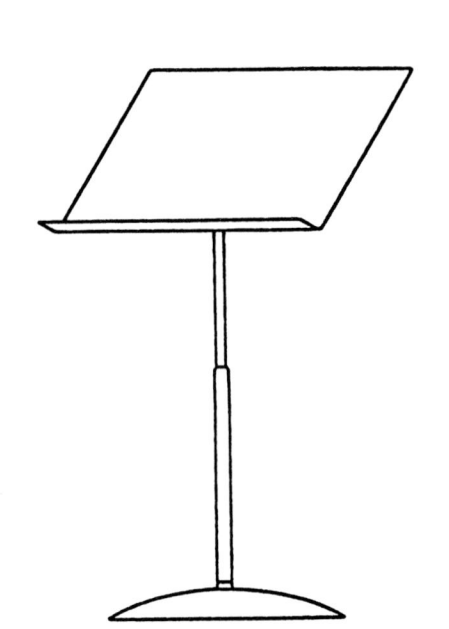

Music Stand:

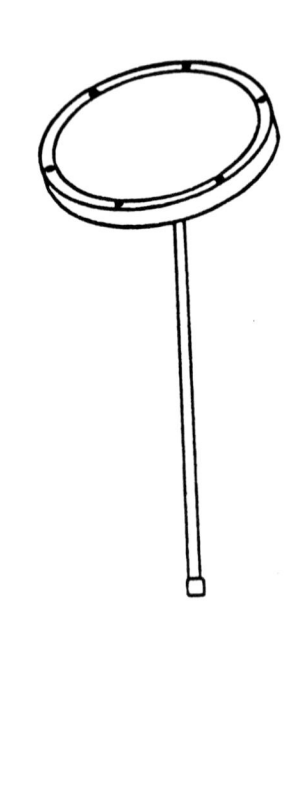

Snare Drum:

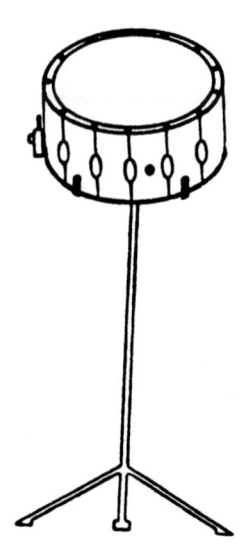

STEP TWO

*** HOLDING THE STICKS ***

THE MATCHED GRIP:

1. The thumb and forefinger grasp the stick about 1/3 from the back (or "butt end") of the drumstick.

2. The stick rests between the first and second knuckle joint of the forefinger.

3. The remaining fingers gently close around the stick.

4. The back of the wrist faces up. Keep the wrist in a horizontal position.

5. The wrist provides the basic stroke. Avoid using the arm.

6. The fingers underneath the stick remain loose and follow the motion of the stick.

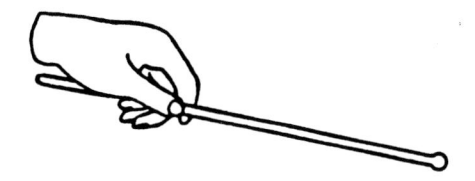

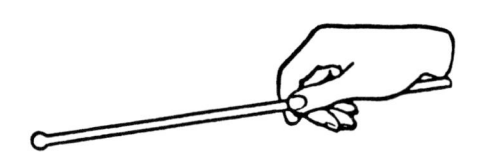

THE TRADITIONAL GRIP: LEFT HAND

1. The stick rests in the fleshy area at the base of the thumb about 1/3 from the "butt end" of the stick.

2. The forefinger and middle finger relax over the stick.

3. The ring finger and little finger relax under the stick. Avoid closing fingers against the hand; keep them in an open position.

4. Pressure should only be exerted by the thumb for the basic stroke.

5. The wrist should be in a vertical position. The wrist motion should rotate for the basic stroke.

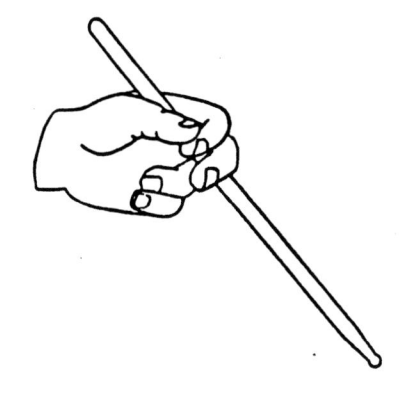

STEP THREE

*** SINGLE STROKES ***

The letter <u>R</u> refers to a stroke with the right hand.

The letter <u>L</u> refers to a stroke with the left hand.

Bounce each stroke <u>off</u> the drumhead or pad.

Notice the numbers 1,2,3,4 on top of each stroke. When playing a stroke, say the accompanying number. This is how we begin to learn to read music.

1.	Count	1	2	3	4	1	2	3	4	1	2	3	4	1	2	3	4
	Play	R	L	R	L	R	L	R	L	R	L	R	L	R	L	R	L
2.	Count	1	2	3	4	1	2	3	4	1	2	3	4	1	2	3	4
	Play	L	R	L	R	L	R	L	R	L	R	L	R	L	R	L	R

The following two exercises are grouped in pairs of two; notice the numbers on top of each stroke are 1 and 2.

3.	Count	1	2	1	2	1	2	1	2
	Play	R	L	R	L	R	L	R	L
4.	Count	1	2	1	2	1	2	1	2
	Play	L	R	L	R	L	R	L	R

The next two exercises are in groups of three; therefore only say the numbers 1, 2, and 3.

5.	Count	1	2	3	1	2	3	1	2	3	1	2	3
	Play	R	L	R	L	R	L	R	L	R	L	R	L
6.	Count	1	2	3	1	2	3	1	2	3	1	2	3
	Play	L	R	L	R	L	R	L	R	L	R	L	R

STEP FOUR

*** DOUBLE STROKES ***

In STEP THREE, the strokes were played in an alternating manner; that is, one hand after another. Now we are going to play strokes by repeating the right and left hands. Do not stop between groups of numbers. Go right on to the next number.

REMEMBER TO COUNT OUT LOUD

1. Count   1 2 3 4   1 2 3 4   1 2 3 4   1 2 3 4
   Play   R R L L   R R L L   R R L L   R R L L

2. Count   1 2 3 4   1 2 3 4   1 2 3 4   1 2 3 4
   Play   L L R R   L L R R   L L R R   L L R R

3. Count   1 2   1 2   1 2   1 2
   Play   R R   L L   R R   L L

4. Count   1 2   1 2   1 2   1 2
   Play   L L   R R   L L   R R

5. Count   1 2 3   1 2 3   1 2 3   1 2 3
   Play   R R R   L L L   R R R   L L L

6. Count   1 2 3   1 2 3   1 2 3   1 2 3
   Play   L L L   R R R   L L L   R R R

7. Count   1 2 3 4   1 2 3 4   1 2 3 4   1 2 3 4
   Play   R R R R   L L L L   R R R R   L L L L

8. Count   1 2 3 4   1 2 3 4   1 2 3 4   1 2 3 4
   Play   L L L L   R R R R   L L L L   R R R R

STEP FIVE

*** IMPROVING OUR STROKE ***

The basic snare drum stroke is executed by the tip of the stick BOUNCING off the drum or pad in the same manner as a ball bounces off the ground.

RULES TO REMEMBER:

Both Grips

1. Allow the stick to rebound off the drum or pad.

2. Avoid forcing the stick into the drum with the wrists.

3. Allow the stick to move within the fingers and hand. It is not correct to grab the stick tightly.

4. Think of holding the snare drum sticks as though you were holding a bird; if you held the bird too tightly it would choke; if you held it too loosely, it would fly away.

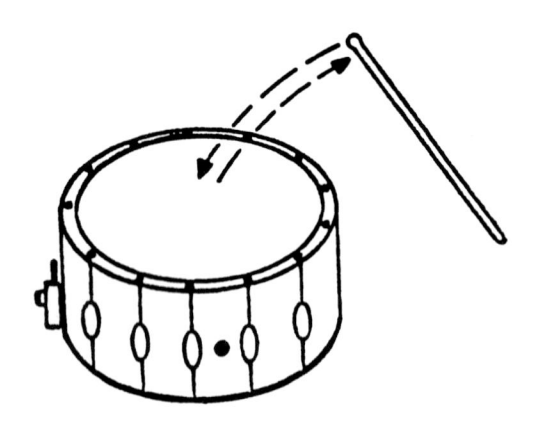

Traditional Grip

5. The two fingers on top of the stick act as a guide. Avoid placing any pressure on the stick from these two fingers. Later, these fingers will be important in the rebound stroke for fast single strokes.

6. Allow the stick to be free of the two fingers beneath the stick when the stick strikes the drum This allows a free *legato* (smooth) stroke which produces the correct sound on the drum.

STEP SIX

Each line twice 9

*** COMBINATIONS OF SINGLE AND DOUBLE STROKES ***

REMEMBER THE RULES FOR CORRECT DRUMMING:

    a. ALLOW EACH STROKE TO BOUNCE OFF THE DRUM OR PAD.
    b. COUNT EACH NUMBER OUT LOUD.

TIME-SIGNATURE

There are two numbers before each line of music. This is called the <u>TIME-SIGNATURE</u>. The top number tells us the amount of beats grouped together which forms a measure. The top number determines how many beats are to be counted. For example, in 4/4 time we count up to four; in 3/4 time, we count up to three; and in 2/4 time we count up to two.

Do not stop between groups of numbers. Go right on to the next number.

```
1.  Count   4    1 2 3 4    1 2 3 4    1 2 3 4    1 2 3 4
    Play    4    R L R L    R R R R    L R L R    L L L L

2.  Count   4    1 2 3 4    1 2 3 4    1 2 3 4    1 2 3 4
    Play    4    R L R L    R R L L    R L R L    R R L L

3.  Count   4    1 2 3 4    1 2 3 4    1 2 3 4    1 2 3 4
    Play    4    R L R L    R L R R    L R L R    L R L L

4.  Count   4    1 2 3 4    1 2 3 4    1 2 3 4    1 2 3 4
    Play    4    R L R L    R L L R    L R L R    L R R L

5.  Count   3    1 2 3      1 2 3      1 2 3      1 2 3
    Play    4    R L L      R L L      R L L      R L L

6.  Count   3    1 2 3      1 2 3      1 2 3      1 2 3
    Play    4    L R R      L R R      L R R      L R R

7.  Count   2    1 2 1 2    1 2 1 2    1 2 1 2    1 2 1 2
    Play    4    R L R R    L R L L    R L R R    L R L L

8.  Count   2    1 2 1 2    1 2 1 2    1 2 1 2    1 2 1 2
    Play    4    R L L R    L R R L    R L L R    L R R L
```

STEP SEVEN

*** LEARNING TO READ QUARTER-NOTES ***

Instead of reading the R and L markings, now let's read the actual notes. A QUARTER-NOTE will be placed under the right and left hand markings.

Top number   4 = number of beats in each measure

Bottom number   4 = which note receives one count

Quarter-Note   ♩ ← Stem   = one count
                            ← Note Head

Each note represents one stroke of the drum stick. Be sure to play every note correctly with one bounce of the stick. COUNT OUT LOUD.

A BAR LINE is a vertical line that separates each measure on the staff. Notice that each BAR LINE separates each group of notes into measures.

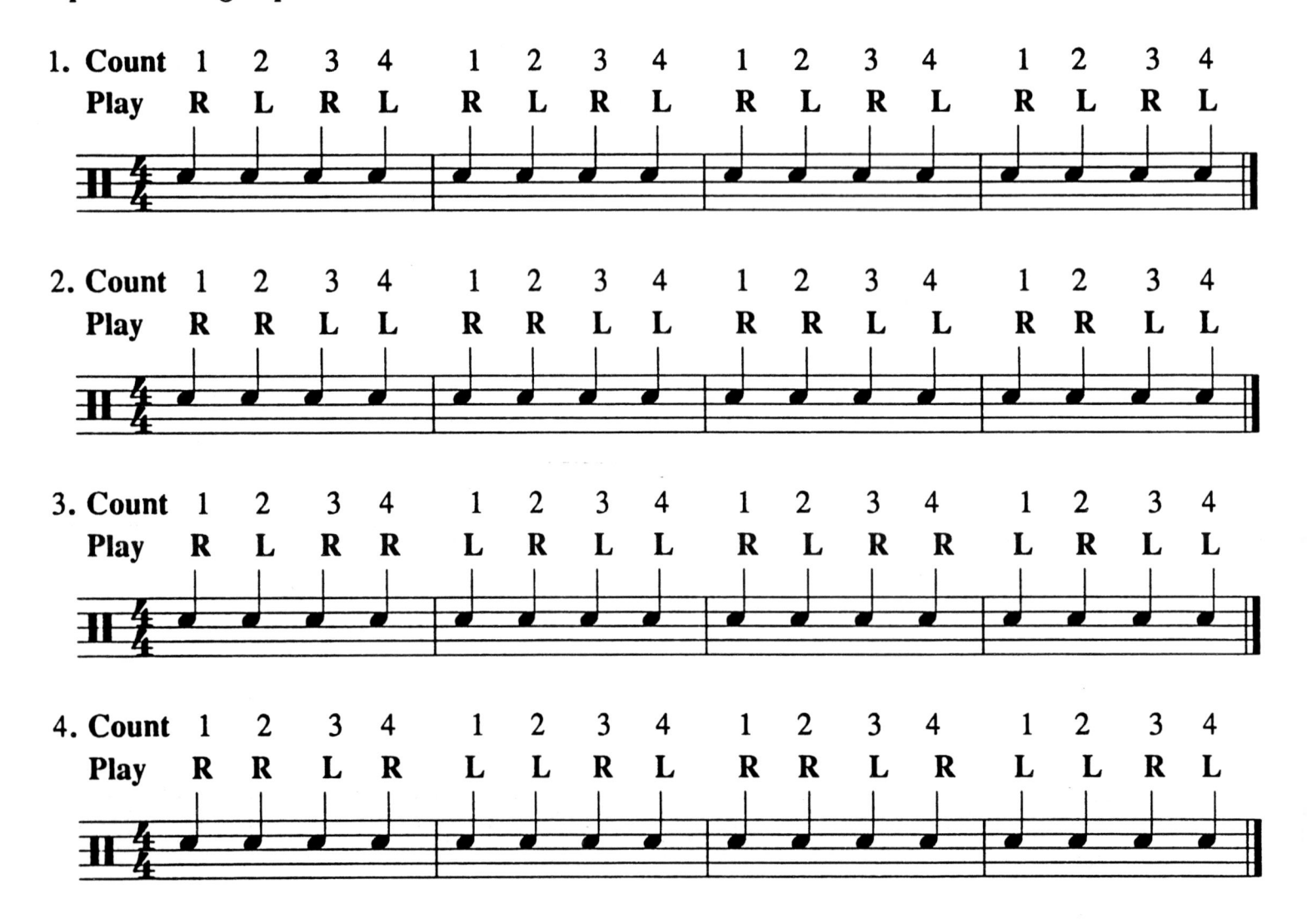

1. Count 1 2 3 4   1 2 3 4   1 2 3 4   1 2 3 4
    Play   R L R L   R L R L   R L R L   R L R L

2. Count 1 2 3 4   1 2 3 4   1 2 3 4   1 2 3 4
    Play   R R L L   R R L L   R R L L   R R L L

3. Count 1 2 3 4   1 2 3 4   1 2 3 4   1 2 3 4
    Play   R L R R   L R L L   R L R R   L R L L

4. Count 1 2 3 4   1 2 3 4   1 2 3 4   1 2 3 4
    Play   R R L R   L L R L   R R L R   L L R L

5. Count 1 2 3 | 1 2 3 | 1 2 3 | 1 2 3
   Play R L R | L R L | R L R | L R L

6. Count 1 2 3 | 1 2 3 | 1 2 3 | 1 2 3
   Play R L R | L L L | L R L | R R R

7. Count 1 2 | 1 2 | 1 2 | 1 2 | 1 2 | 1 2 | 1 2 | 1 2
   Play R L | R L | R L | R L | R L | R L | R L | R L

The next two exercises are in 5/4 time. That means there are 5 beats in a measure. Each quarter-note gets the count. Simply count up to five for each measure.

8. Count 1 2 3 4 5 | 1 2 3 4 5 | 1 2 3 4 5 | 1 2 3 4 5
   Play R L R L R | L R L R L | R L R L R | L R L R L

9. Count 1 2 3 4 5 | 1 2 3 4 5 | 1 2 3 4 5 | 1 2 3 4 5
   Play R L R R R | L R L L L | R L R R R | L R L L L

The final exercise is in 6/4. What does the 6 mean?

10. Count 1 2 3 4 5 6 | 1 2 3 4 5 6 | 1 2 3 4 5 6 | 1 2 3 4 5 6
    Play R L R L L R | L R L R R L | R R R L L L | R R R L L L

STEP EIGHT

*** QUARTER-RESTS ***

𝄽 = **One count of silence.**

For every note value there is an equivalent rest. The QUARTER-REST is counted for one beat just as the quarter-note.

A REST MEANS "DON'T PLAY".

Now let's play some exercises combining quarter-notes and quarter-rests.

1. Count 1 2 3 4 | 1 2 3 4 | 1 2 3 4 | 1 2 3 4
   Play R L R L | R   L | R L R L | R   L

2. Count 1 2 3 4 | 1 2 3 4 | 1 2 3 4 | 1 2 3 4
   Play R L R | L R L | R L R L | R L R

3. Count 1 2 3 4 | 1 2 3 4 | 1 2 3 4 | 1 2 3 4
   Play R   L | R L R L | R   L | R L R L

4. Count 1 2 3 4 | 1 2 3 4 | 1 2 3 4 | 1 2 3 4
   Play   R L | R L R | L   R | L R L

5. **Count** 1 2 3 4 1 2 3 4 1 2 3 4 1 2 3 4
Play R L R L R L R L R L R L

6. **Count** 1 2 3 1 2 3 1 2 3 1 2 3
Play R L R L R L R L

7. **Count** 1 2 3 1 2 3 1 2 3 1 2 3
Play R L R L R L R L R L

8. **Count** 1 2 3 1 2 3 1 2 3 1 2 3
Play R L R L R L R L R

9. **Count** 1 2 3 4 5 1 2 3 4 5 1 2 3 4 5 1 2 3 4 5
Play R L R L R L R L R L R L R L R L

10. **Count** 1 2 3 4 5 1 2 3 4 5 1 2 3 4 5 1 2 3 4 5
Play R L R L R L R L R L R L R L

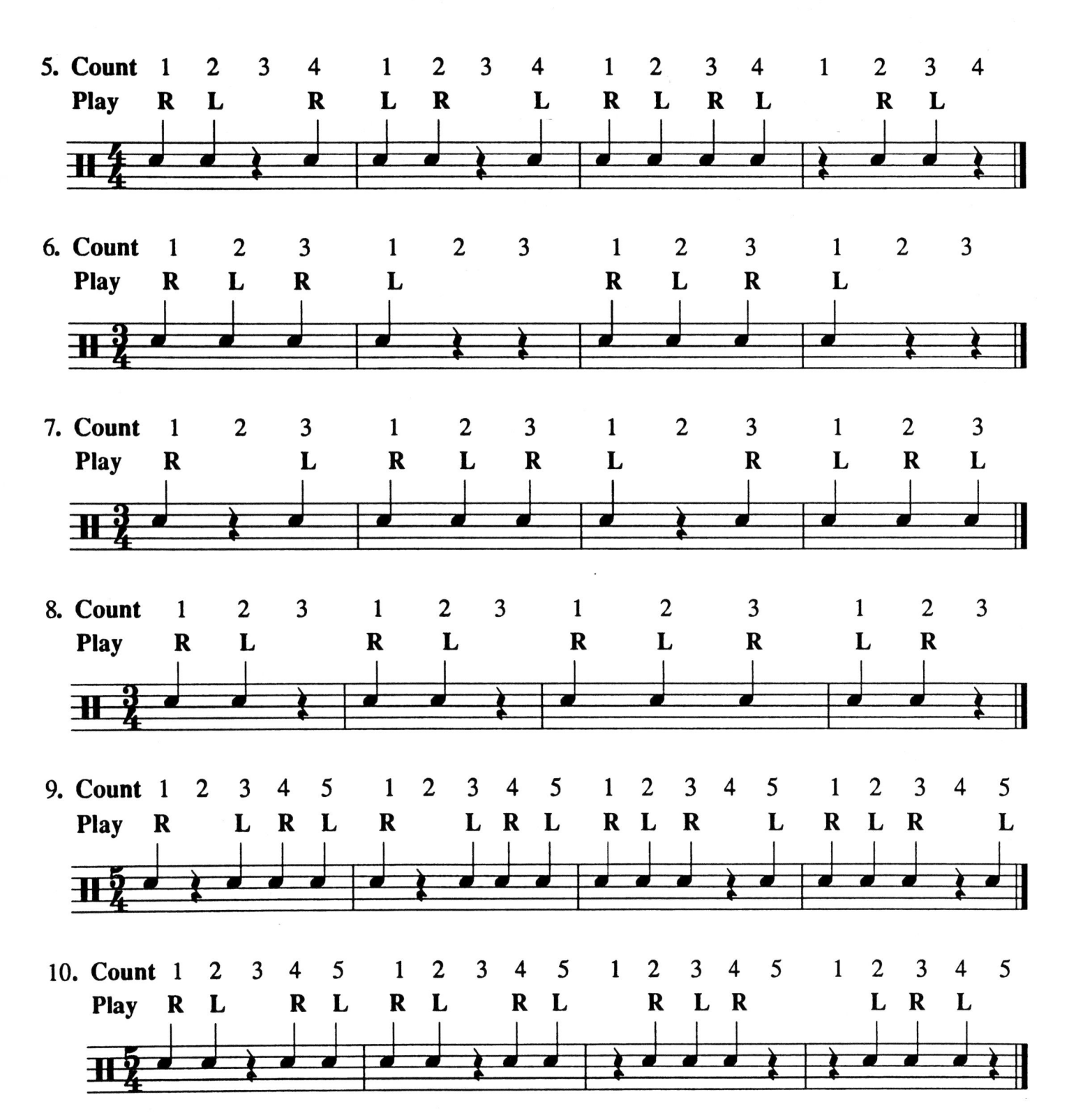

STEP NINE

*** BASS DRUM ***

The BASS DRUM is used in most percussion music. It provides the lowest sound in the percussion family and functions as the "heart beat" of the band or orchestra with its steady rhythmic pulse. The BASS DRUM part is usually written on the 1st space of the staff with the stem down.

TUNING THE BASS DRUM

The BASS DRUM should be tuned as low as possible; but never so low that the sound is loose or flabby. The non-playing head may be tuned lower than the playing head. Turn the lugs in pairs evenly around the drum. Never use any external or internal devices to muffle the sound of the drum.

GRIPPING THE BASS DRUM MALLET

The BASS DRUM mallet is held with the right hand. Grip it securely using the entire hand.

THE PROPER BEATING SPOT

The mallet should strike the drum slightly below center (not halfway between the center and the edge). The center area produces the lowest and most resonant quality on the BASS DRUM.

THE PROPER STROKE

Strike the drum in the correct beating spot with a direct blow to the head. Always strike off the head allowing the stroke to follow through. Do not glance off the head in an up and down motion.

Use large wrist strokes when playing loud and smaller strokes when playing soft. The slower the tempo, the slower the preparation and follow through.

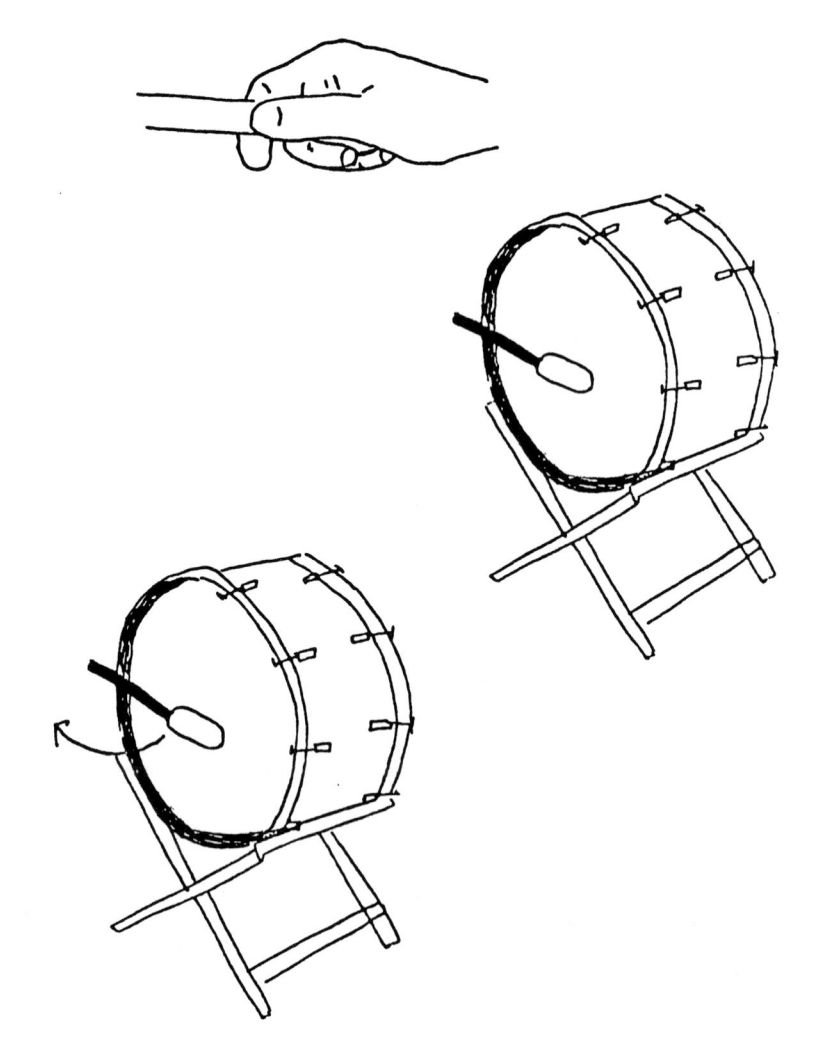

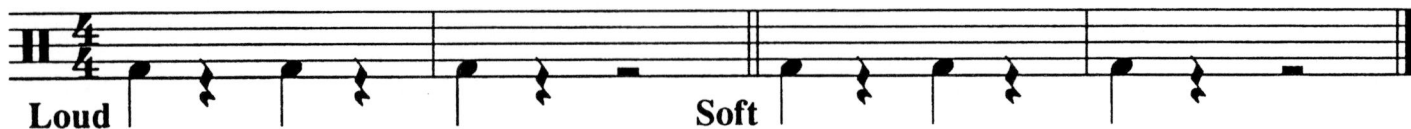

Loud   Soft

MUFFLING

The technique for producing a very short note on the BASS DRUM is as follows:

1. Strike the drum in the proper manner with the right hand.

2. The right knee muffles the playing head.

3. The left hand muffles the non-playing head.

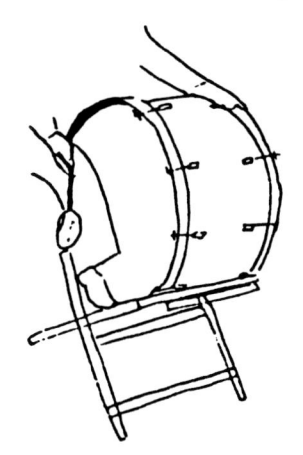

The performer's right foot should rest on the bass drum stand if possible; if not, balance on the left foot and lift the right knee up to the head.
This allows the right hand to remain free to strike the drum and not to be involved in the muffling process.

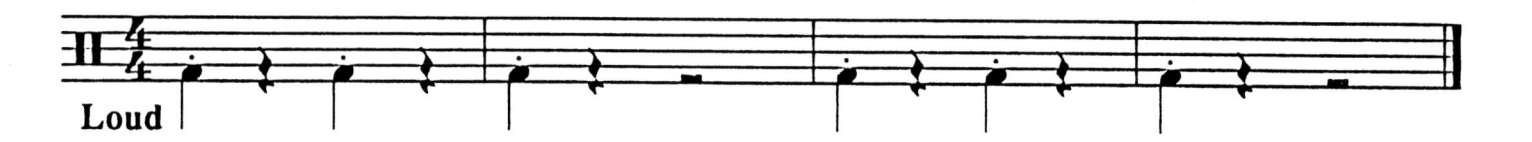

Loud

CONTROLLING BASS DRUM RESONANCE

Many times, the sound of the BASS DRUM is too resonant for the musical ensemble. An unfortunate solution to this problem is to have an external or internal muffler attached to the drum head. The problem with this solution is that the drum can no longer produce a full resonant sound when needed.

The correct procedure for controlling resonance is to have the left (non-playing) hand reach over and muffle the playing head. The amount of pressure will determine the muffling effect.

Damping to an even greater degree is accomplished by using the right knee on the playing head and the left hand on the non-playing head. NEVER MUFFLE THE NON-PLAYING HEAD BY ITSELF. This will destroy the low fundamental sound of the drum.

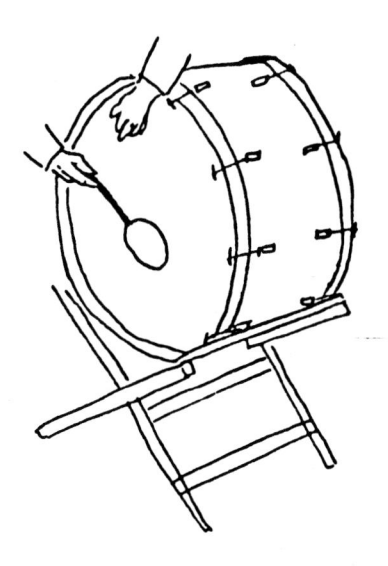

STEP TEN

*** SNARE DRUM SOLOS ***

Now let's put more measures together and produce longer pieces which we call solos. A few standard rules apply to these pieces and for most exercises in the book.

The rules are as follows:

1. ALTERNATE THE STROKES: The general rule for playing snare drum solos is to alternate by using a different hand for each stroke.

2. START WITH YOUR STRONGEST HAND: Right-handed players should begin each piece with the right hand, and vice versa for left-handed players.

3. ALWAYS COUNT OUT LOUD: This rule is very important. Every beat of the measure, including the rests, must be counted.

4. TAP YOUR FOOT ON EACH BEAT (OPTIONAL): The foot (right or left) may tap on every beat, including the rests.

5. REBOUND OFF THE PAD OR DRUMHEAD: It is important to execute every stroke in the proper manner. Do not press the stick into the drumhead; let it bounce off like a ball.

MY FIRST SOLO

The bass drum is added to help make the sound complete, although each part may be practiced independently.

A QUICK STEP

GIVE ME FIVE

MOVING ALONG

WALTZ FOR ONE

STEP ELEVEN

*** HALF-NOTES AND WHOLE-NOTES ***

We can combine different numbers of beats to form longer-sounding notes. For example, the value of two, quarter-notes equals one, half-note.

One, half-note equals two beats.

The value of four, quarter-notes equals one, whole-note.

One, whole-note equals 4 beats.

Each of these notes has an equivalent rest.

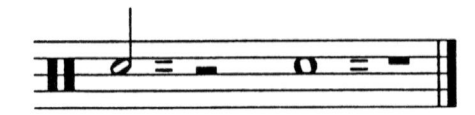

The half-rest sits on the third line (it isn't so heavy); the whole-rest hangs from the fourth line (it has more weight). Strike each note only one time while counting the proper numbers of beats.

Half-Notes

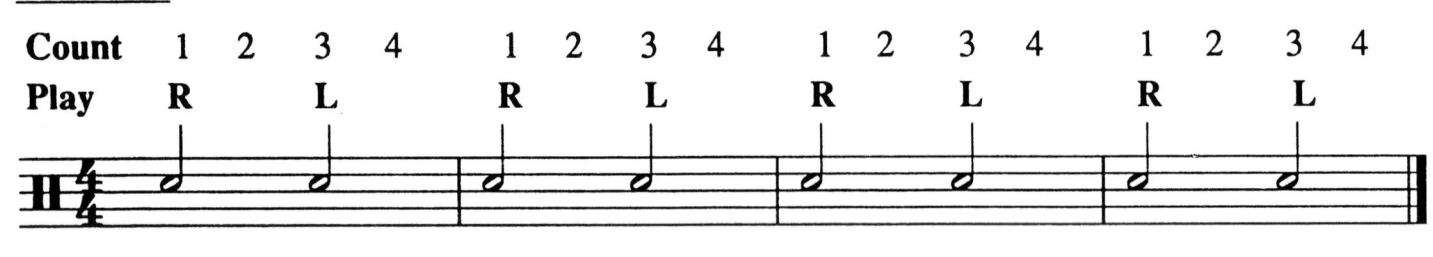

Count	1	2	3	4	1	2	3	4	1	2	3	4	1	2	3	4
Play	R		L		R		L		R		L		R		L	

Whole-Notes

Count	1	2	3	4	1	2	3	4	1	2	3	4	1	2	3	4
Play	R				L				R				L			

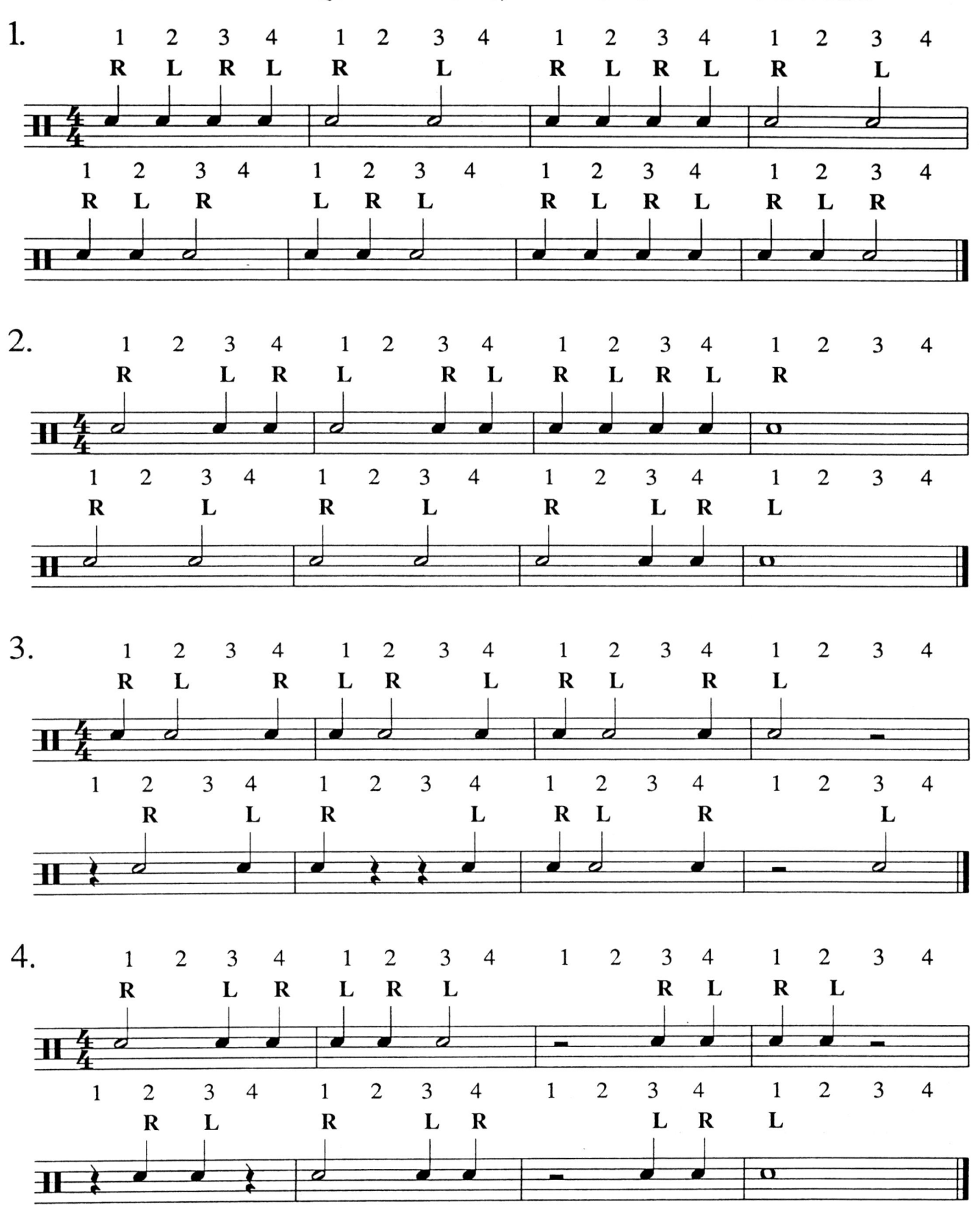

COMBINATIONS OF QUARTER-NOTES, HALF-NOTES AND WHOLE-NOTES

STEP TWELVE

*** CRASH CYMBALS ***

CRASH CYMBALS are also used quite often in percussion writing. When a part is marked "Cymbals" it usually refers to CRASH CYMBALS.

The cymbal part can be written on the first space along with the bass drum part or indicated by an X (or a normal note) on a separate line.

A pair of 18" CRASH CYMBALS is a good size for most situations. For elementary school bands, a smaller pair of 14" or 16" will suffice.

THE PROPER GRIP

Use cymbals with leather straps; never use a wooden handle. A small felt pad on the dome of the cymbal will help to cushion the knuckles against the instrument.

The following is the correct procedure for holding the CRASH CYMBALS:

1. Place the leather strap inside the hand.

2. Grasp the strap firmly with the thumb and forefinger.

3. The tip of the thumb should press against the cymbal providing a secure grip.

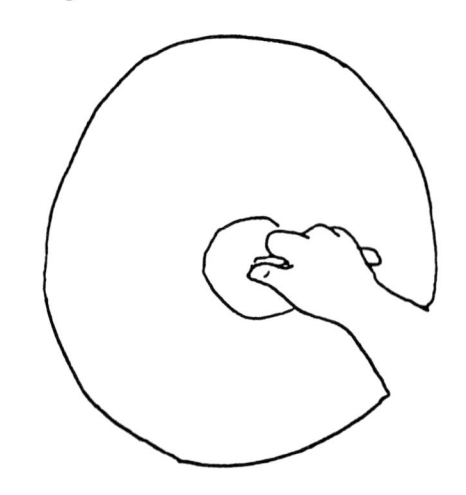

THE LOUD CRASH

The following is the correct procedure for playing a loud crash:

1. Grasp the straps as described.

2. The stronger hand is held above the other. (Right-handed players hold the right cymbal above the left.)

3. The cymbals are held at a slight angle to each other.

4. The upper cymbal strikes the lower cymbal in a downward motion. The bottom edges striking first, then the top.

5. After they are struck together, hold them up to sustain the sound.

ACCOMPANIMENT TECHNIQUE

Most of the music for CRASH CYMBALS is not written as loud crashes, but as steady rhythms as in a March. Any pattern of notes other than loud crashes are played as follows:

1. The right-hand cymbal strikes the left-hand cymbal about one inch below the top.

2. The left-hand remains stationary while the right-hand strikes in a downward motion. Never strike with an up-and-down motion.

3. The strokes do not have to be very large. The idea is to produce repeated strokes which are as similar as possible.

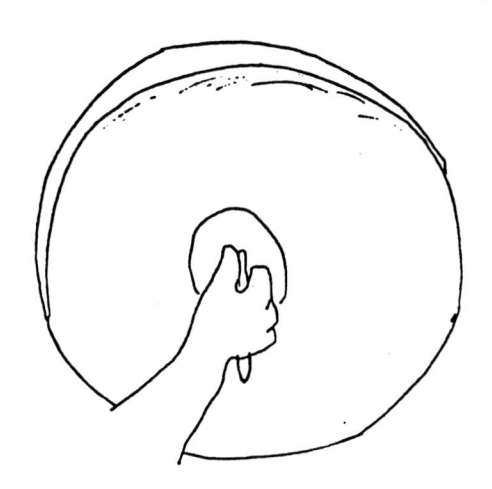

MUFFLING

Muffling is important to control the cymbal's enormous sound. After a crash, pull the cymbals to your shoulders to stop the sound, For simple muffling after softer dynamics, stop the sound by holding the cymbals against your stomach.

SUSPENDED CYMBAL

The SUSPENDED CYMBAL is mounted on a stand and played with mallets. The percussion part will usually indicate when this cymbal should be used. Whether the part is marked SUSPENDED CYMBAL or not, it is normally used for rolling and rhythmical figures.

MALLETS

Percussion parts do not always indicate what type of mallet to use when striking the cymbal. A medium yarn or cord mallet (such as a vibraphone mallet) can be used for most parts. There are times when a snare drum stick will work better; for example when the part is loud and short.

STRIKING THE SUSPENDED CYMBAL

When using yarn mallets, strike the SUSPENDED CYMBAL near the edge.

When using a snare drum stick, strike the SUSPENDED CYMBAL on the edge with the butt end of the stick.

ROLLING

Use two yarn mallets to produce a roll. Keep the mallets near the edge of the SUSPENDED CYMBAL for the best sound. Use single strokes to roll on the SUSPENDED CYMBAL.

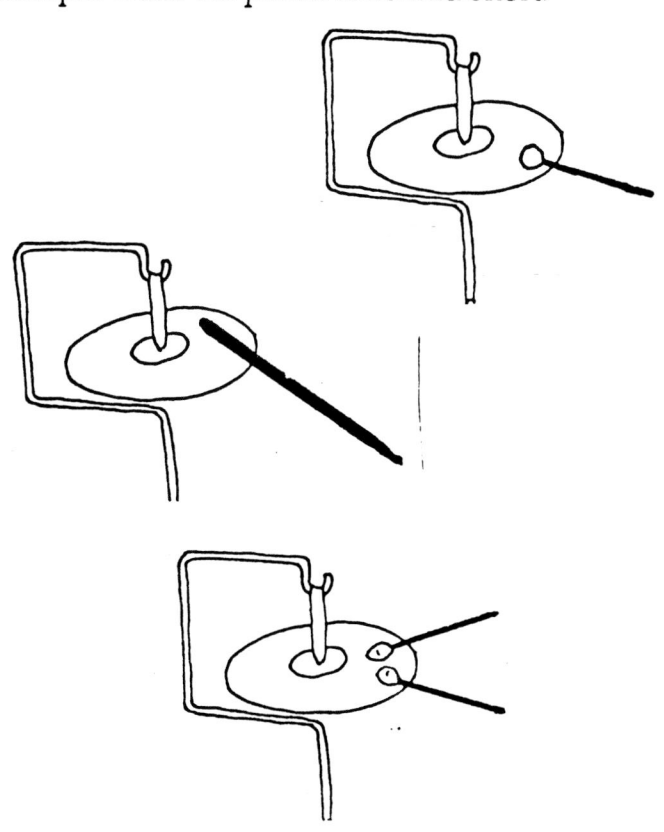

STEP THIRTEEN

*** DRUM SOLOS WITH QUARTER, HALF AND WHOLE-NOTES ***

Bass Drum and Crash Cymbals should now play the notes on the first space in unison. Remember to count out loud and alternate sticking.

LONG NOTE MARCH

ONE EXTRA BEAT

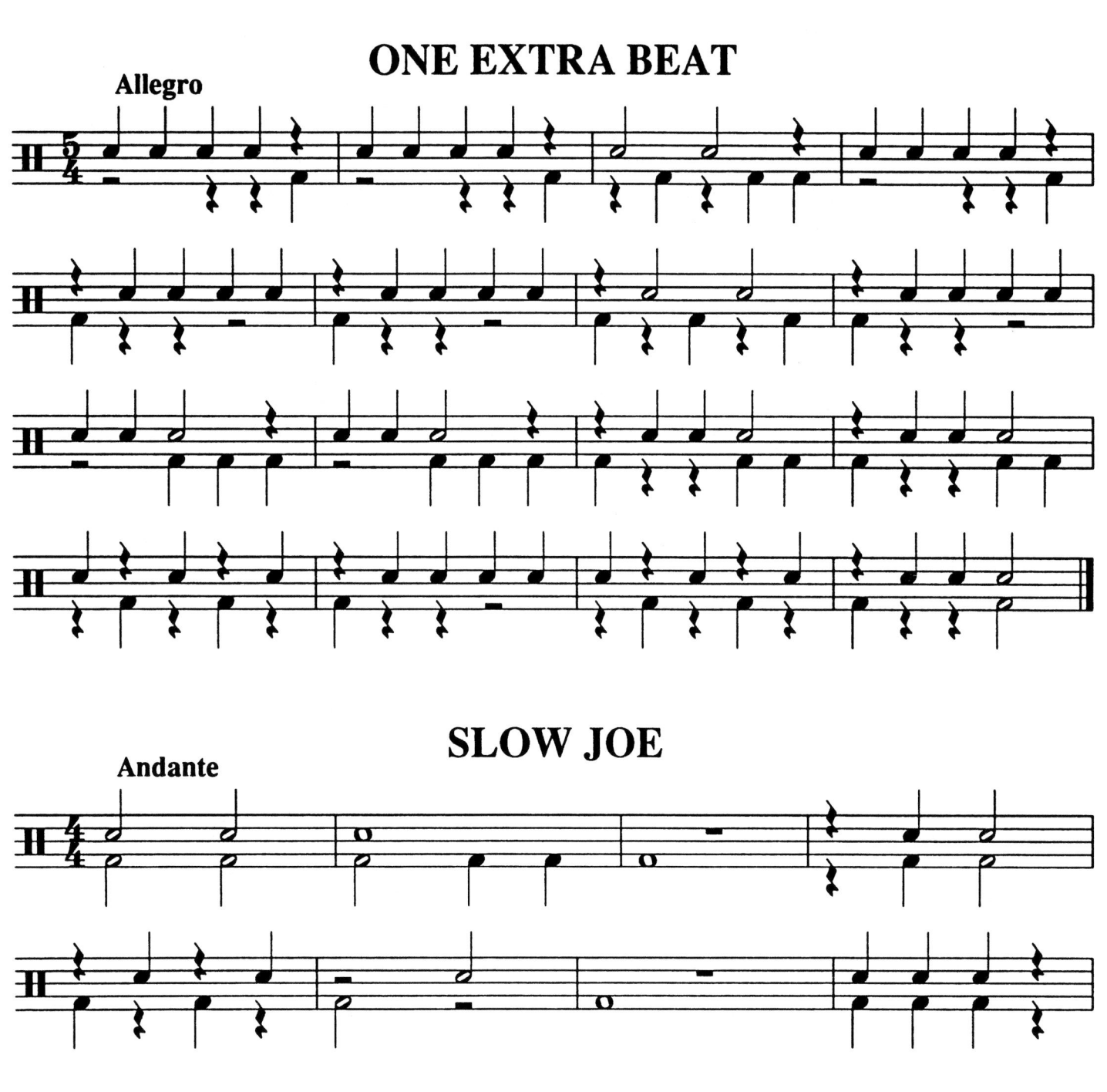

Allegro

SLOW JOE

Andante

STEP FOURTEEN

*** DOTTED HALF-NOTES ***

A dot after a half-note or half-rest increases the value of that note or rest by 1/2.

Since the value of a half-note is two beats.......
A DOTTED HALF-NOTE equals three beats.

*** THE REPEAT SIGN ***

The addition of two dots at the end of a double bar tells us to go back to a double bar with similar dots placed on the inside of the bar, or to return to the beginning of the piece.

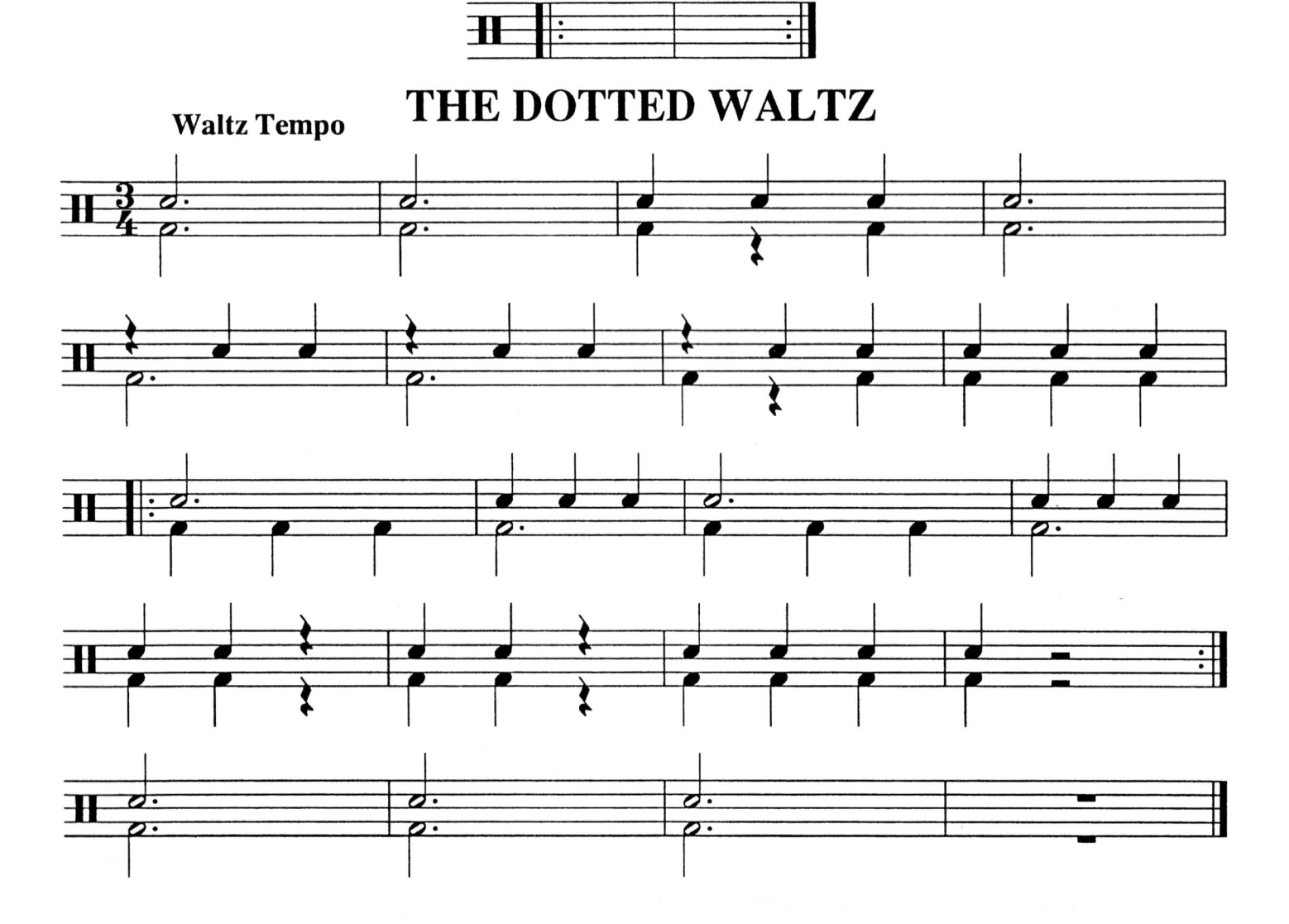

THE DOTTED WALTZ

Waltz Tempo

f = Loud p = Soft

This solo will introduce 1st and 2nd endings.

MOVING RIGHT ALONG

Allegro

SIX BEAT CAPER

Andante

STEP FIFTEEN

*** EIGHTH-NOTES ***

A single EIGHTH-NOTE has a flag and looks like this:

When two EIGHTH-NOTES are played one after the other, they are joined at the top by a beam.

One quarter-note equals two EIGHTH-NOTES.

One half-note equals four EIGHTH-NOTES.

One whole-note equals eight EIGHTH-NOTES.

EIGHTH-NOTES are counted by using the word <u>AN</u>. A group of EIGHTH-NOTES in 4/4 time is counted as follows:

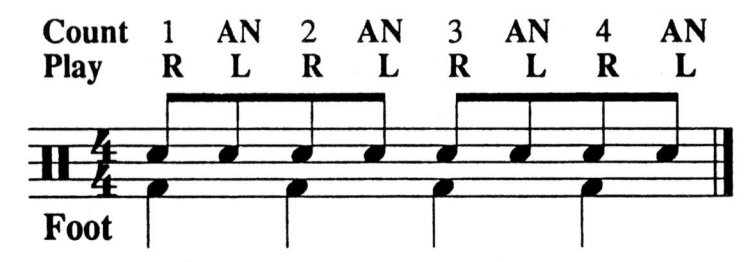

```
Count  1  AN  2  AN  3  AN  4  AN
Play   R  L   R  L   R  L   R  L
```

Foot

The foot may be tapped on the main beats; that is, the 1, 2, 3, and 4 counts.
Do not tap the foot on <u>AN</u>.

The exercises on this page use eighth-note patterns that are connected with beams. Single eighth-notes will be introduced later.

Practice the following combinations of eighth and quarter-notes. This sticking is for a right-handed player; left-handed players should reverse the sticking patterns.

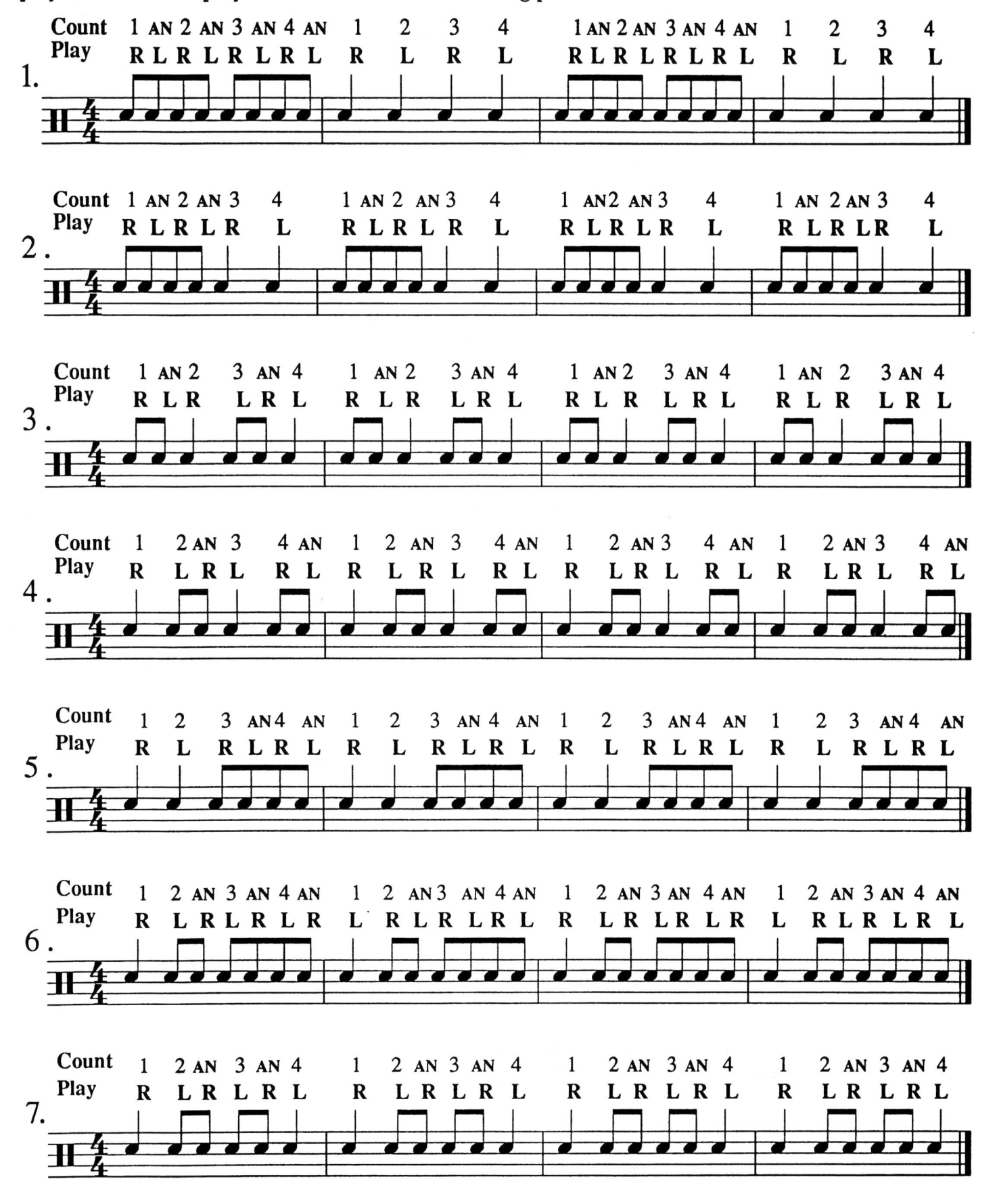

STEP SIXTEEN

*** DRUM SOLOS WITH EIGHTH-NOTES ***

Tap your foot on the main beats of the measure.

SKIPPING ALONG

IN THE GROOVE

THREE STEPS

FIGURE THIS OUT

STEP SEVENTEEN

*** THE SNARE DRUM ROLL ***

We are now going to learn how to play a snare drum roll. The purpose of the roll is to sustain the sound over the value of a written note.

The first exercise is called the BOUNCE STROKE. This stroke is different from the single stroke because it contains more than one bounce. Using the same motion of the wrist, bounce the stick on the drum or pad a number of times not just once.

Rules for playing the BOUNCE STROKE:

1. Strike the drum in the same manner as for a single stroke.

2. Do not change the way you hold the stick.

3. Increase the pressure on the thumb and forefinger to produce the multiple-bounce stroke. (when using traditional grip, the left-hand pressure is increased at the base of the thumb.)

4. Multiple bounces should be fairly close together. It doesn't matter how many bounces are produced; but, there must be more than two.

THE BOUNCE STROKE

Once the desired sound is produced, increase the speed of the bounce stroke until a continuous sound is heard.

Practice the following exercise SLOW to FAST:

Slow ---------------- to ---------------- Fast

QUARTER-NOTE ROLLS

Begin the roll on the count of ONE and end it on the count of TWO.
A slur indicates the roll is tied into the final note without a break in the sound.

Play the quarter-note at the end of the roll as a SINGLE STROKE not as a BOUNCE STROKE.

```
Count  1 2   1 2   1 2   1 2
Play   R R   L L   R R   L L
```

The tempo (how fast or slow the music is played) determines the length of a roll. For example, a quarter-note roll in a slow tempo takes much longer than a quarter-note roll in a fast tempo. Therefore, more bounce strokes are needed for rolls in slower tempos than fast tempos.

For now, practice all rolls in a slow tempo.

HALF-NOTE ROLLS

Begin the roll on the count of ONE and end it on the count of THREE.

```
Count  1 2 3 4   1 2 3 4   1 2 3 4   1 2 3 4
Play   R   R     L   L     R   R     L   L
```

WHOLE-NOTE ROLLS

Begin the roll on the count of ONE and end it on the count of ONE in the next measure.

```
Count  1 2 3 4   1 2 3 4   1 2 3 4   1 2 3 4
Play   R         R         L         L
```

STEP EIGHTEEN

*** DRUM SOLOS WITH ROLLS ***

Rules to remember when playing rolls:

1. Each ROLL is made up of multiple-bounce strokes.
   These strokes produce a sustained sound called a ROLL.
   Each bounce-stroke should contain more than two bounces.

2. When a solo begins with a ROLL, start the ROLL with your strongest hand. During the solo however, alternate the strokes.

3. Play the note at the end of the ROLL as a single stroke. Do not use the bounce stroke for this note.

ROLLING ALONG

ROLLING IN THE MORNING

A SWEET ROLL

STEP NINETEEN

*** THE TRIANGLE ***

The TRIANGLE is one of the standard percussion instruments used in the Band or Orchestra. It adds a beautiful, ringing, metallic sound to the music.

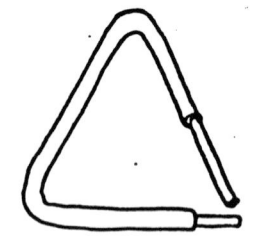

THE TRIANGLE HOLDER

The TRIANGLE clip or holder is pictured at the right. It consists of a clothespin-type clip with a gut or plastic string looped under the center area which holds the TRIANGLE. Do not use yarn or soft string.

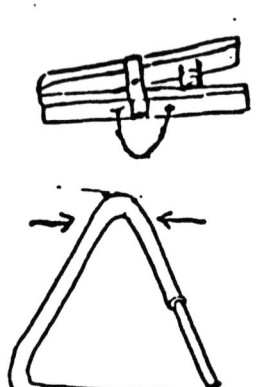

THE PROPER BEATING SPOT

Different sounds are produced in various areas of the TRIANGLE. Strike the TRIANGLE wherever it sounds best. The normal beating spots are opposite the top and side angles.

HOLDING THE TRIANGLE

Hold the TRIANGLE clip in the left hand, resting the bottom of the clip on your thumb and middle fingers. The forefinger rests on top of the clip and the remaining two fingers are held away from the TRIANGLE.

THE PROPER STROKE

Strike the TRIANGLE so the beater falls onto the metal surface. Do not try to snap the beater off the TRIANGLE with a quick stroke; this procedure can, very easily, result in missing the TRIANGLE completely.

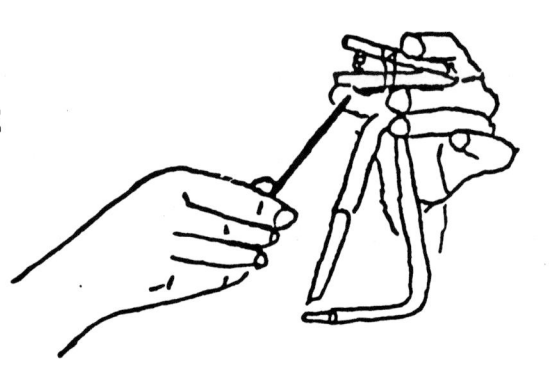

THE TRIANGLE ROLL

To roll or sustain a sound on the TRIANGLE, quickly move the beater from side to side. The roll can either be produced inside the top angle or between the side angles. For soft dynamics, roll close to the angle; for louder dynamics move the beater away from the angle and more into the center area.

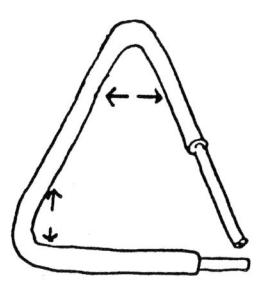

COMBINING SINGLE STROKES AND ROLLS

Play all single strokes on the outside of the TRIANGLE. The rolls are played on the inside of one of the angles. The end of the roll is also played on the inside.

The following music is an example using combinations of rolls and single strokes.

PERFORMING RAPID STROKES

When a composer writes a part that is too fast for one hand to play, place the TRIANGLE on a stand and use two beaters. If a TRIANGLE stand is not available, use a music stand.

Clip the TRIANGLE to the stand striking the top angle with both beaters. Rolls can also be played in this manner.

STEP TWENTY

*** THE FLAM ***

Snare drum rudiments are the fundamental techniques of drumming. This lesson introduces the FLAM, one of many drum rudiments. Every rudiment contains certain groups of notes with special sticking patterns. The name of the sound that is produced when two strokes strike the drum very close together is called a FLAM.

A FLAM is notated by a small note attached to a regular note.

The name of the FLAM is determined by the hand that plays the regular (larger) note.

Right-Handed Flam:

L **R**

Left-Handed Flam:

R **L**

The correct procedure for playing a Flam is as follows:

1. For a right-handed flam, the right hand is held in the up position and the left hand in the down position. (Diagram A)

2. Both hands are then released at the same time. The hand in the down position should hit the drum slightly before the hand in the up position.

3. For a left-handed flam, the left hand is held in the up position and the right hand in the down position. (Diagram B)

4. When a right-handed flam is followed by another right-handed flam, the right hand returns to the up position. If a right-handed flam is to be followed by a left-handed flam, the left hand returns to the up position.

Diagram A 						Diagram B

THE FLAM AND STROKE

When a flam is followed by a series of single strokes, the correct sticking pattern is to ALTERNATE the strokes.

When two or more flams are written, the correct sticking is to use the SAME FLAM. The idea is to produce the same sound in a consistent manner.

There are times when it is necessary to alternate flams. The following exercise develops alternating flams.

STEP TWENTY ONE

*** THE FLAM TAP AND FLAM ACCENT ***

THE FLAM TAP

The FLAM TAP is another snare drum rudiment. The FLAM TAP consists of a right flam followed by a right stroke and a left flam followed by a left stroke.

THE FLAM ACCENT

The FLAM ACCENT consists of a right flam followed by two alternating strokes plus a left flam followed by two alternating strokes.

The normal sticking pattern for flams and strokes is to alternate the strokes as shown below:

*** FLAM STUDIES ***

The standard rule for drumming is to ALTERNATE STROKES. The following exercises demonstrate the use of this rule with single strokes and flams.

Observe the sticking and COUNT OUT LOUD.

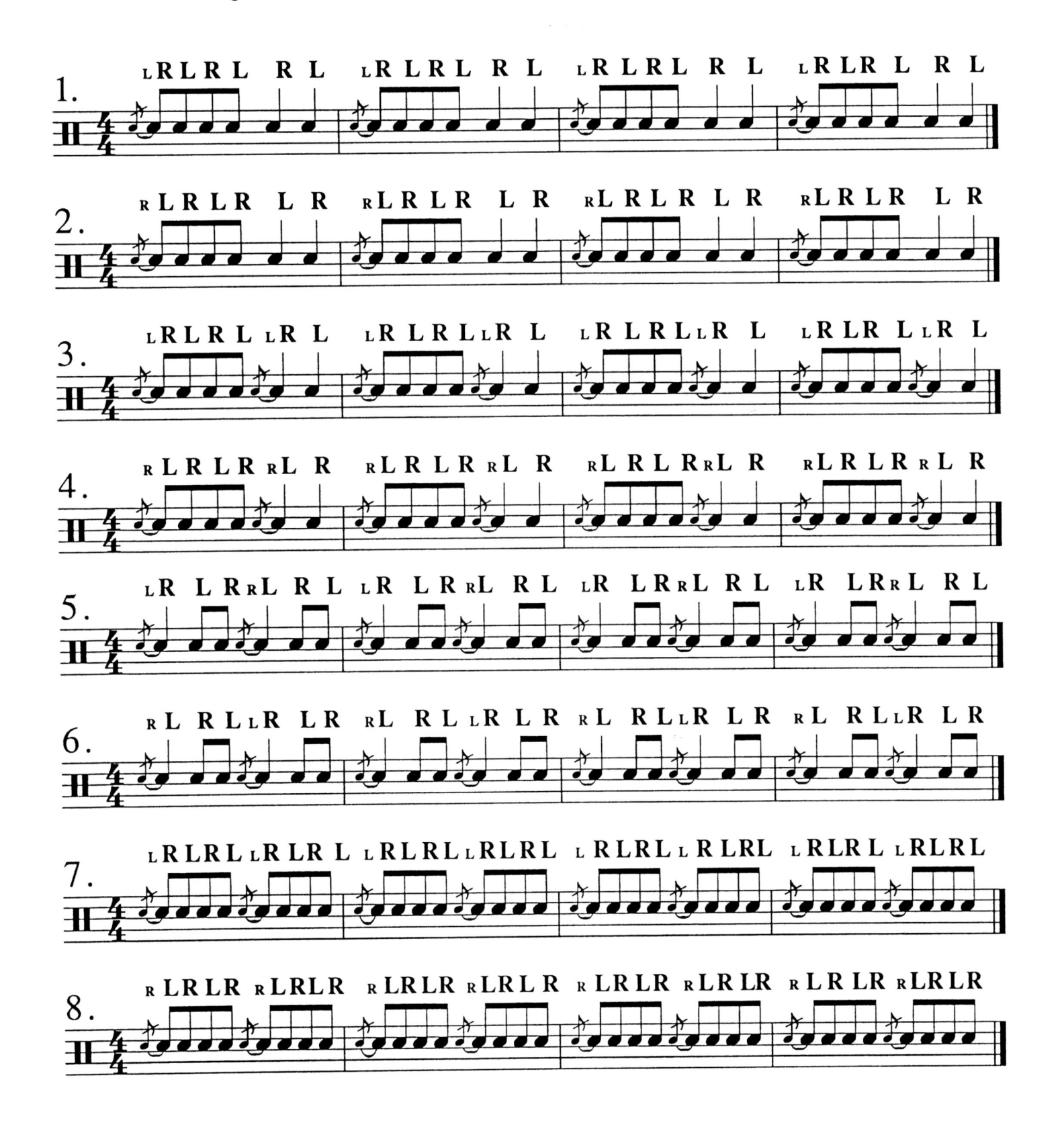

STEP TWENTY TWO

*** SIX-EIGHT TIME ***

All of the music up to now has been written in 2/4, 3/4, 4/4, 5/4 or 6/4 time. The top number of the time-signature indicates the number of beats in a measure. The bottom number indicates which note value gets one count. Therefore, all of the previous time-signatures indicated that the quarter-note value got one count.

> 4 - Indicates the number of beats in a measure.
> 4 - Indicates which note value gets one count.

When we change the bottom number (4) to an 8, this now indicates that the eighth-note value will get one count. The top number still tells us how many beats are in the measure.

> 6 - Indicates six beats to a measure.
> 8 - Indicates the eighth-note gets one count.

Six-eight time, because it works so well in writing marches, is the most common of the "eight" time-signatures. Now, practice the following exercises in six-eight time. Remember, COUNT OUT LOUD.

Just as we added a dot to a half-note in Volume One, we can add a dot to a quarter-note to increase its value by 1/2.

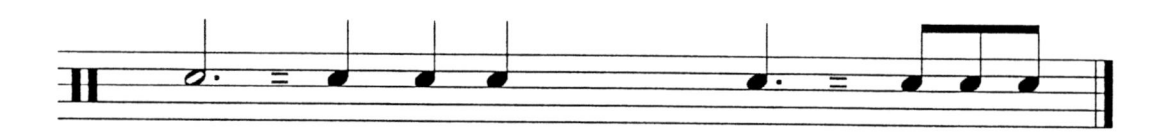

A dotted quarter-note will now get three counts in 6/8 time.

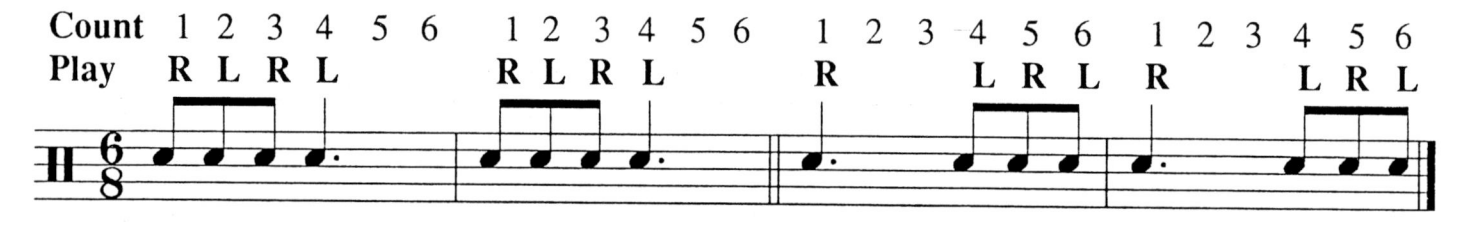

An EIGHTH-REST gets 1/2 beat, just like an eighth-note. In six-eight time, the EIGHTH-REST gets one count.

EXERCISES IN SIX-EIGHT TIME

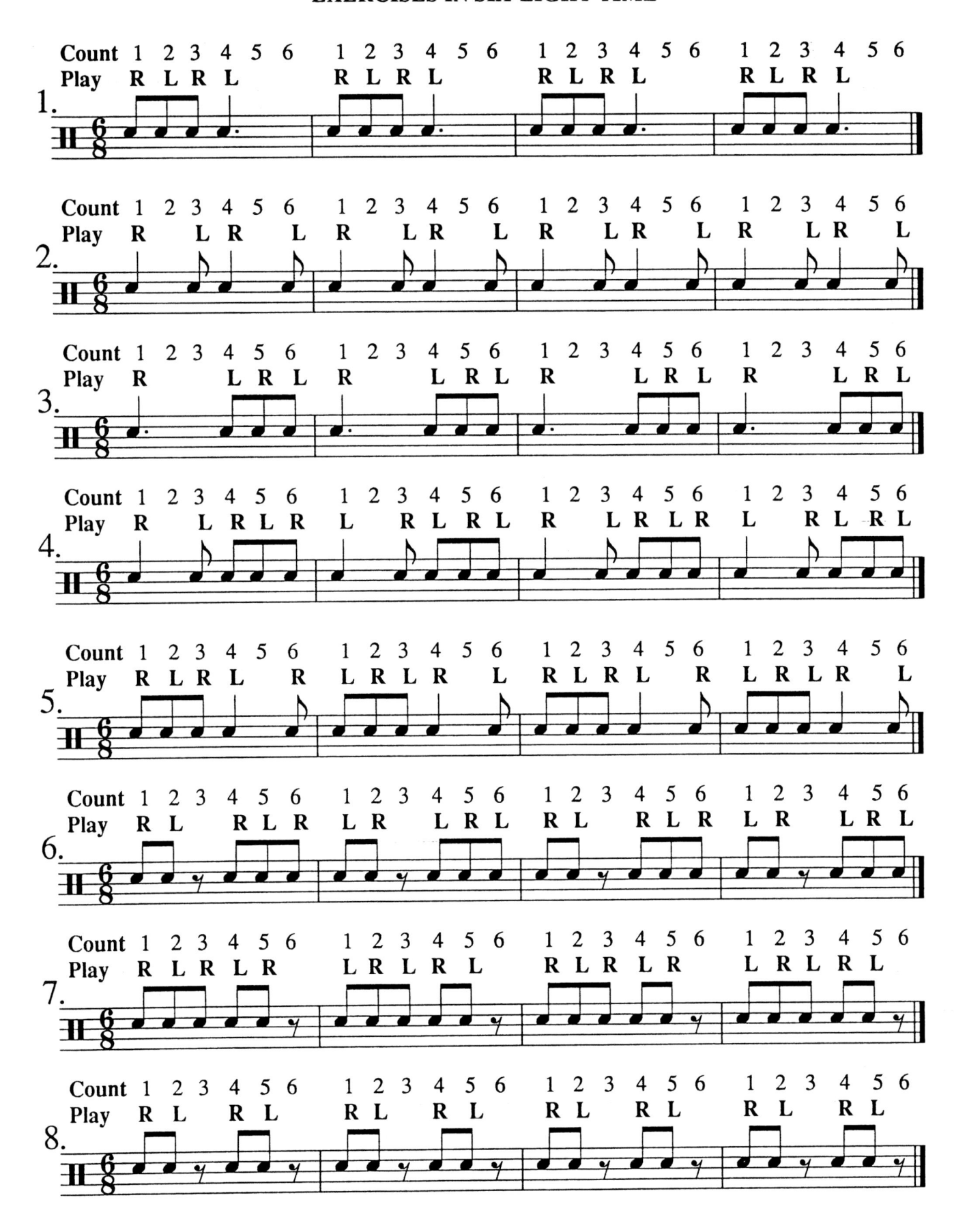

1. Count: 1 2 3 4 5 6 | 1 2 3 4 5 6 | 1 2 3 4 5 6 | 1 2 3 4 5 6
Play: R L R L | R L R L | R L R L | R L R L

2. Count: 1 2 3 4 5 6 | 1 2 3 4 5 6 | 1 2 3 4 5 6 | 1 2 3 4 5 6
Play: R L R L R L R L | R L R L R L R L | R L R L R L R L | R L R L R L R L

3. Count: 1 2 3 4 5 6 | 1 2 3 4 5 6 | 1 2 3 4 5 6 | 1 2 3 4 5 6
Play: R L R L R | L R L R | L R L R | L R L

4. Count: 1 2 3 4 5 6 | 1 2 3 4 5 6 | 1 2 3 4 5 6 | 1 2 3 4 5 6
Play: R L R L R L | R L R L R L | R L R L R L | R L R L R L

5. Count: 1 2 3 4 5 6 | 1 2 3 4 5 6 | 1 2 3 4 5 6 | 1 2 3 4 5 6
Play: R L R L R | L R L R L | R L R L R | L R L R L

6. Count: 1 2 3 4 5 6 | 1 2 3 4 5 6 | 1 2 3 4 5 6 | 1 2 3 4 5 6
Play: R L R L R L R | L R L R L | R L R L R | L R L R L

7. Count: 1 2 3 4 5 6 | 1 2 3 4 5 6 | 1 2 3 4 5 6 | 1 2 3 4 5 6
Play: R L R L R | L R L R L | R L R L R | L R L R L

8. Count: 1 2 3 4 5 6 | 1 2 3 4 5 6 | 1 2 3 4 5 6 | 1 2 3 4 5 6
Play: R L R L | R L R L | R L R L | R L R L

STEP TWENTY THREE

*** DRUM SOLOS IN SIX-EIGHT TIME ***

For classroom instruction, the triangle can now also play the top line by simply eliminating any flams.

STRAIGHT EIGHT

OFF BEAT CAPER

ROLLING IN 6/8

ATTENTION MARCH

STEP TWENTY FOUR

*** DRUM SOLOS WITH ROLLS AND FLAMS ***

FLAM AND STROKE

FLAM TAP AND FLAM ACCENT

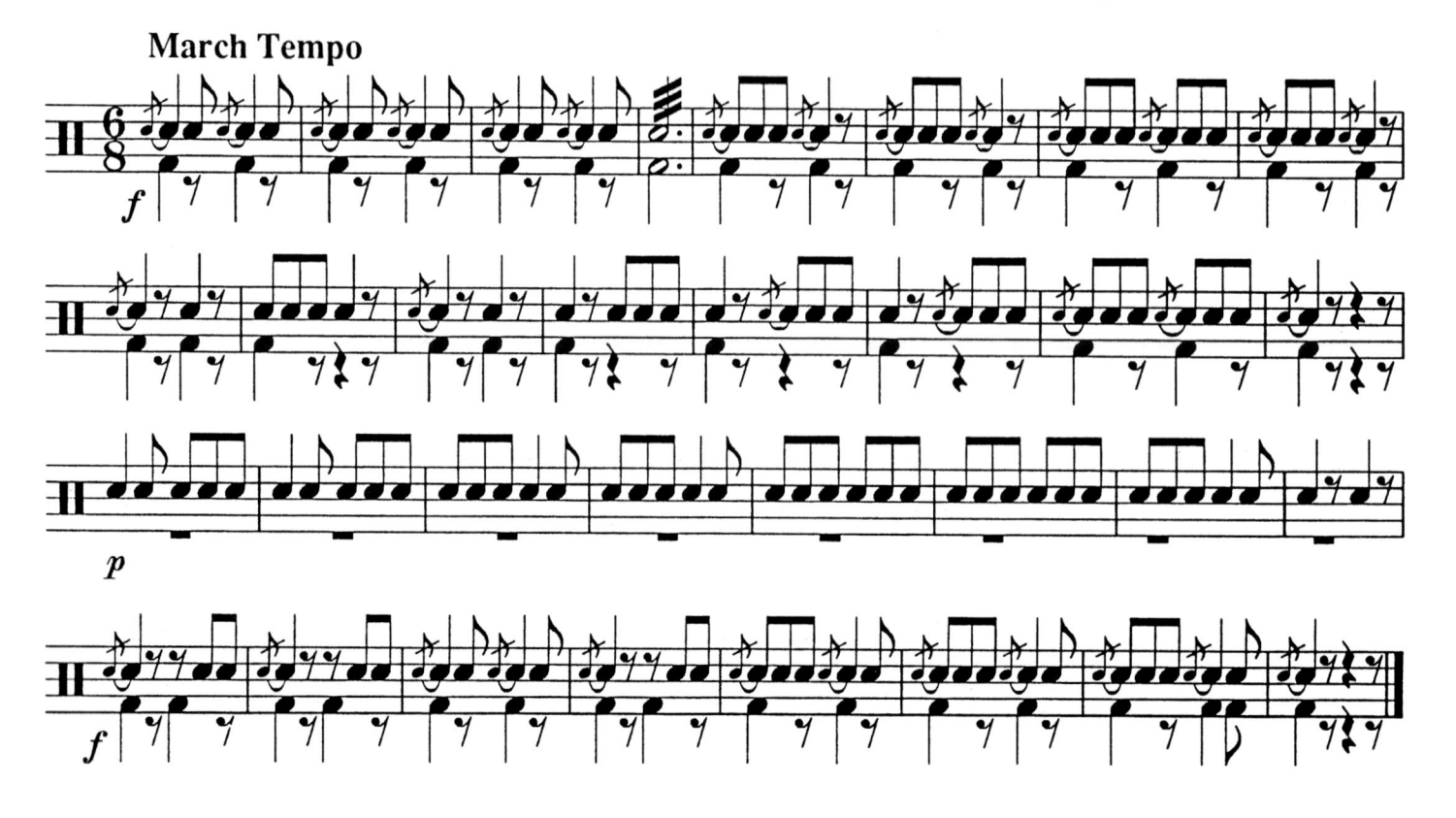

The accent mark (>) means to strike that note louder.

QUESTION AND ANSWER SOLO

FLAM WALTZ

STEP TWENTY FIVE

*** THE TAMBOURINE ***

The proper TAMBOURINE for a band or orchestra consists of a wooden shell with two rows of jingles and a calf-skin head. Avoid using tuneable tambourines with plastic heads.

HOW TO PLAY THE TAMBOURINE

1. Right-handed players should hold the TAMBOURINE in the left hand by grasping the shell in the area where the jingles have been removed.

2. The thumb secures the grip by firmly grasping the head.

3. Hold the TAMBOURINE at a slight angle so the jingles are at rest. Do not hold the TAMBOURINE in a vertical position when playing (the jingles will rattle).

4. The right hand can then be used for striking the head.

The following techniques are used when a single note or a series of notes are slow enough to be played by one hand:

THE LOUD STROKE

1. To play a series of loud notes, strike the head in the center with the flat area of the knuckles, using a wrist motion.

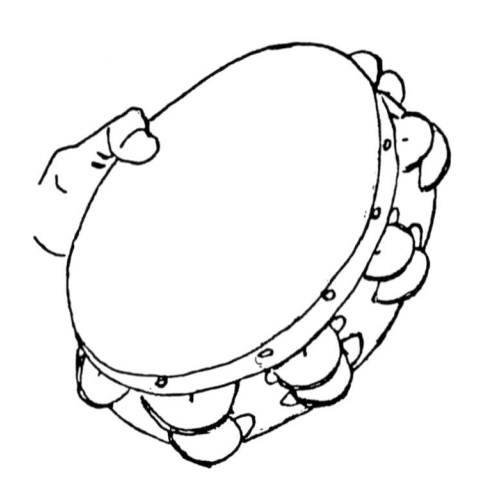

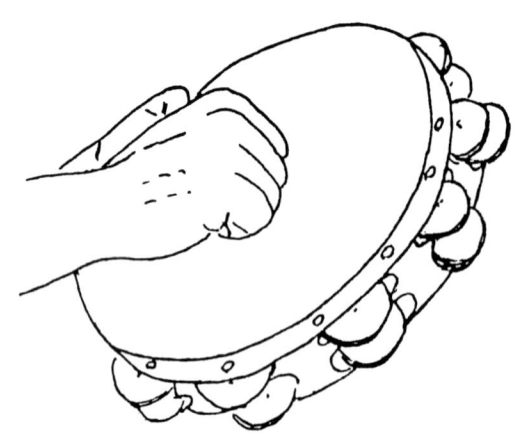

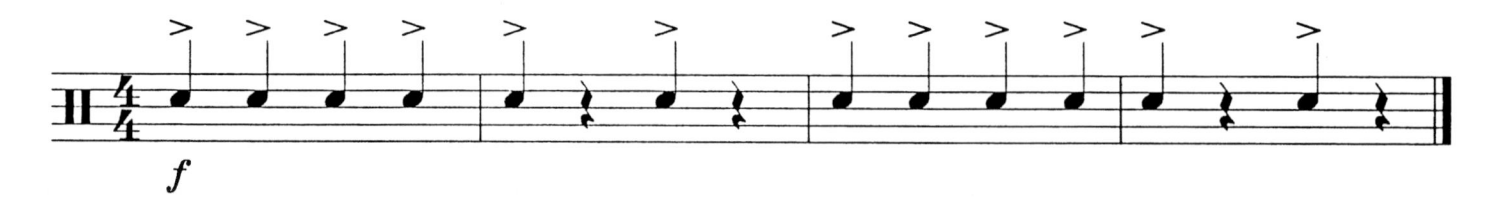

THE SOFT STROKE

1. To play a series of soft notes on the TAMBOURINE, strike the head near the rim with the finger tips.

2. Do not use the center area of the head for soft strokes.

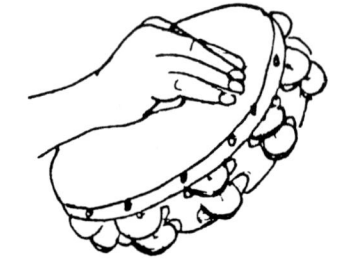

THE LOUD ROLL

1. To perform a loud roll, hold the TAMBOURINE in the left hand as before and rotate the wrist to shake the jingles and produce a sustained sound.

2. Start and end each roll with a stroke.

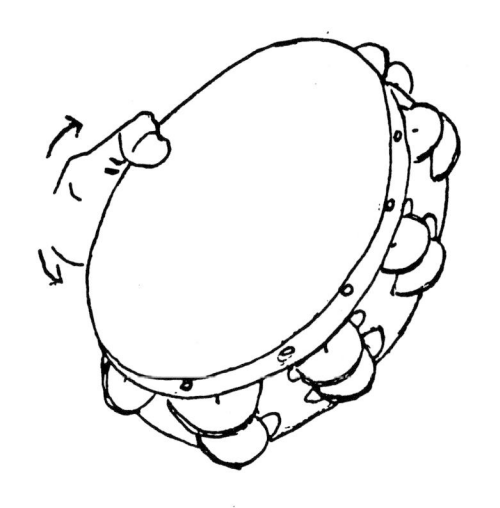

THE SOFT ROLL

1. To produce a soft roll, rub the tip of your thumb around the perimeter of the TAMBOURINE.

2. Moisten the tip of your thumb with your tongue in order to obtain enough friction to vibrate the jingles.

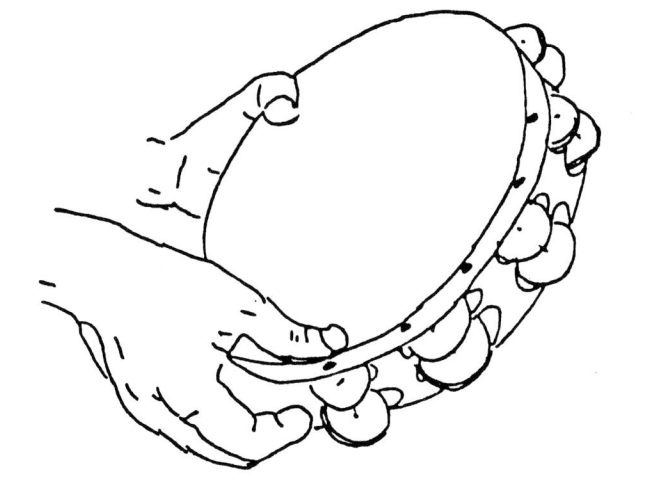

It is important to be aware of the amount of noise a TAMBOURINE makes whenever it is moved. Always place the instrument down carefully and avoid all excess noise!

STEP TWENTY SIX

*** CUT-TIME ***

The time-signature of 4/4 is sometimes indicated as C (common time). The time-signature of CUT-TIME is indicated by ¢. CUT-TIME means that instead of the quarter-note receiving one beat, the measure is divided into two beats, thereby giving the half-note one beat.

In both cases, the notation is exactly the same. The difference lies in where the rhythmic emphasis is placed. In 4/4 time, the four beats are relatively equal. In CUT-TIME, there are only two pulses in the measure (the first and third beats). CUT-TIME is useful when the tempo moves along very quickly.

CUT-TIME may be counted in the normal four beats to the measure or it may be counted in two (as in 2/4).

Ex. 1: Counting in four.   Ex. 2: Counting in two.

Now let's try some solos in CUT-TIME.
Count the following solos in four (as in Ex. 1).

For classroom instruction, the tambourine can now also play the top line by eliminating the flams.

CUT-TIME MARCH

Fermata - Hold this note longer.

FORWARD MARCH

Moderato

TRAVELLING FAST

Allegro

STEP TWENTY SEVEN

SNARE DRUM SOLOS

Review STEP TWENTY for the proper stickings.

MARCHING ALONG

THREE'S COMPANY

SIX-EIGHT MARCH

ONE MORE BEAT

STEP TWENTY EIGHT

*** SIXTEENTH-NOTES ***

A single SIXTEENTH-NOTE has two flags and looks like this:

When two SIXTEENTH-NOTES are played one after the other, they are joined at the top by two beams.

One eighth-note equals two SIXTEENTH-NOTES.

One quarter-note equals four SIXTEENTH-NOTES.

One half-note equals eight SIXTEENTH-NOTES.

SIXTEENTH-NOTES are counted in the following manner:

```
COUNT   1 E AN DA   2 E AN DA   3 E AN DA   4 E AN DA
PLAY    R L R  L    R L R  L    R L R  L    R L R  L
```

The foot may only be tapped on the main beats; that is, the 1, 2, 3, and 4 counts.

*** SIXTEENTH-NOTE EXERCISES ***

STEP TWENTY NINE

*** FINAL SNARE DRUM SOLOS ***

RHYTHM ROMP

EASY MOVE

4/4 FOR FUN

THE END